# Spy Files

# SPY SCHOOL

FIREFLY BOOKS

# A FIREFLY BOOK

Published by Firefly Books Ltd. 2009
Copyright © 2008 QEB Publishing, Inc.

Words in **bold** can be found in the glossary on page 30.

First printing

Publisher Cataloging-in-Publication Data (U.S.)
Gilbert, Adrian.
    Spy files: spy school / Adrian Gilbert.
[32] p. : photos. (chiefly col.).  ;  cm.
Summary: Focuses on the different types of spies, their training techniques, including fake identities and disguises, surveillance, following people, and intelligence. Includes case histories of famous spies.
ISBN-13: 978-1-55407-575-1 (pbk.)
ISBN-10: 1-55407-575-0 (pbk.)
1. Secret service – Juvenile literature.  2. Spies – Training of – Juvenile literature.  I. Title.
327.12 dc22    HV7961.G55 2009

A CIP record for this book is available from Library and Archives Canada.

Published in the United States by
Firefly Books (U.S.) Inc.
P.O. Box 1338, Ellicott Station
Buffalo, New York 14205

Published in Canada by
Firefly Books Ltd.
66 Leek Crescent
Richmond Hill, Ontario L4B 1H1

Printed and bound in China

**Author** Adrian Gilbert
**Consultant** Clive Gifford
**Editor** Amanda Askew
**Designer** Lisa Peacock
**Picture Researcher** Maria Joannou

**Publisher** Steve Evans
**Creative Director** Zeta Davies

**Picture credits** (t=top, b=bottom, l=left, r=right)
**Alamy Images** Ianni Dimitrov 19t
**Corbis** Ann Thomas 20t, Bettmann 6t, 18, 28t, 28b, Blaine Harrington III 21b, Hulton-Deutsch Collection 11, 27b, Jeffrey L Rotman 17t, Owen Franken 21t, Roger Ressmeyer 7, Ron Sachs/CNP 6b, Sygma 12t, 14r, 15b
**DK Images** Geoff Dann 16, 24t
**Getty Images** Daniel Berehulak 5, General Photographic Agency 23, Geoffrey Manasse/Time Life Pictures 27t, Herbert Orth/Time Life Pictures 10, HO/AFP 15t, Kurt Hutton/Picture Post/Hulton Archive 22t, Nicholas Kamm/AFP 13, Popperfoto 9b, Scott Nelson/AFP 22b, Tim Sloan/AFP 12b
**Istockphoto** 20b
**Mary Evans Picture Library** Rue des Archives 8
**Photoshot** UPPA 26
**Rex Features** Kip Rano 17b, Philippe Hays 24b, Roger-Viollet 9t, 25, Sipa Press 29
**The International Spy Museum** 14l
**Topham Picturepoint** 4b, Metro-Goldwyn-Mayer Pictures /Columbia Pictures/EON Productions 4t, Universal Pictures 19b

# Contents

# Spy recruitment

**The last person an** intelligence **organization would normally want to employ is a spy like James Bond.**

According to **MI5**, a spy should be able to blend into the background. When recruiting secret agents, MI5 looks for average height, build, and appearance. Male applicants should be no taller than 5 feet 9 inches, and female applicants should be no taller than 5 feet 5 inches.

▲ *James Bond in action—a secret agent better suited to the movies than real-life **espionage**.*

Western intelligence organizations are always on the look out for recruits with good language skills. Popular language choices include Russian, Chinese and, more recently, Arabic.

▲ *Richard Sorge (1895–1841) was a brilliant Soviet spy, who used his knowledge of several languages when working undercover.*

Organizations such as MI5 and the **CIA** used to secretly invite people to become spies, but now they advertise in newspapers and on their websites.

➤ *An ad for the British secret service (**MI6**), intended to widen the scope of recruits to MI6.*

Secret agents working in foreign countries will try to use local people working for the **government**. The agent may offer them money in exchange for secret information.

## Top Secret!

Until recently, British intelligence used to recruit many of its spies from the universities of Oxford and Cambridge — but so too did Soviet Intelligence!

# LEGALS AND ILLEGALS

Spies in a **hostile country** are divided into "legals" and "illegals." Legals work from the **embassy** in the foreign country and they have **diplomatic status**, so that if caught, they will normally be returned to their home country. They are fairly easy for the foreign country's security service to spot.

Illegals take on false identities and work on their own or in a small team. They are harder to catch, but if caught, they have no diplomatic status, and may be imprisoned, or tortured and executed.

# Spy training

**Major intelligence organizations, such as the CIA, KGB and MI6, provide thorough training for their agents.**

Spy training—or **tradecraft** as it is more usually called— is very demanding because it calls for many different skills.

◄ In this exercise from World War II, British soldiers are trained to notice if German spies have disguised themselves as mothers with babies.

Spies need to know the tricks of their trade, such as taking secret photographs and setting up **dead drops**, as well as being good at dealing with people.

► President George W. Bush visits a U.S. secret service training center to see dog handlers at work.

Spies will be instructed in how to recruit other agents in a foreign country, and how to encourage them to provide valuable secret intelligence. Knowledge of foreign languages is considered to be very important, as are various types of self-defense.

Other skills they are taught include setting up meetings, following a suspect and learning how to avoid being tailed. By the end of the course, the trainee will be well on the way to becoming a proper secret agent.

▲ Knowledge of martial arts, such as Tae Kwon Do, is encouraged by the CIA.

## Top Secret!

Trainee secret agents are often asked to perform difficult tasks in real-life situations. CIA trainees are sent to the town of Norfolk, Virginia, to practice their spying skills on the local people.

## CAMP PEARY

The CIA has its own special training center, Camp Peary near Williamsburg in Virginia. Nicknamed "the Farm," agents are instructed in survival training, how to use radios, write reports, **interrogate** suspects and resist interrogation themselves.

# Types of spy

There are many different kinds of spy. A handler **will manage several spies who each provide information. Sometimes a** courier **is needed to physically transfer this information. Women have traditionally made good couriers because they were less likely to be searched.**

**Defectors** — people who leave their country to work for another — are highly effective as they usually bring valuable information with them. Igor Gouzenko worked in **Soviet** intelligence and when he defected to the **West** in 1945, he was able to tell the CIA and MI6 about Soviet spies in North America.

Oleg Penkovsky was a double agent, working for the Soviet Union and the West at the same time.

## DOUBLE AGENTS

**Double agents**, such as Oleg Penkovsky, are even more useful than defectors. Penkovsky remained at his post as a KGB officer, while providing the West with high-quality intelligence. The role of a double agent is dangerous—Penkovsky was caught, interrogated and shot by the KGB.

# ASSASSINS

KGB agent Ramón Mercader tracked down Soviet ruler Joseph Stalin's rival, Leon Trotsky, and killed him with an ice pick in Mexico in 1940. Bogdan Stashinsky, another KGB agent, **assassinated** anti-Soviet Ukrainians in West Germany during the 1950s with a poison gas spray hidden in a newspaper.

◄ KGB assassin Ramón Mercader lies in a in hospital bed, after being wounded by Trotsky's guards.

# CELEBRITY SPY

A singer and dancer in Paris before World War II, Josephine Baker was an unlikely spy. After the Germans **occupied** France in 1940, Baker smuggled documents for the French **Resistance**. She used her celebrity status, knowing that the Germans would not think to search such a popular entertainer.

▲ Although born in America, Josephine Baker became a French citizen in 1937 and worked for French intelligence during World War II.

9

# Creating a legend

**Spies operating in a hostile country create a false identity to disguise their spying activities.**

They need a convincing **cover story** about their supposed past life, as well as the right false documents and clothes. A very detailed type of cover is known as a legend. When creating a legend, the spy must have good acting skills. If he lets his mask slip, he is likely to be caught. If, for example, his documents say he has got a limp, then he must limp at all times and with the correct leg.

The various identity cards of Soviet secret agent, Peter Deriakin, who defected to the West.

## FORGERY

During World War II (1939–1945), Britain's **SOE** sent nearly 500 agents into German-occupied France. To help these agents, SOE ran a **forgery** section to produce fake documents, which included passports, travel permits and work passes. To make their forgeries convincing, SOE managed to steal the right papers and inks from France.

# LEGENDARY LONSDALE

From the age of 11, Soviet intelligence prepared Konon Molody for life as a spy. He was sent to live with his aunt in California. After further spy training in the Soviet Union, he was given the name of Gordon Lonsdale, a Canadian citizen.

The real Gordon Lonsdale was born in Canada, but died without family in Finland as a young child. Soviet agents used Lonsdale's birth certificate to secure a passport and other documents. This built a perfect legend for Molody. Posing as a Canadian businessman, the new Lonsdale travelled to Britain and was the handler for several spies working for the KGB.

## Top Secret!

Pocket litter is the name given to the items in a spy's pockets, such as theater tickets, receipts and coins. This makes their cover seem more real.

**Konon Molody
(1922–1970)**

## "Identity Exchange"

**Nationality:** Soviet Union

**Worked for:** KGB

**Life:** He was a handler for several Soviet spies in Britain, and worked to find secrets about the Royal Navy's underwater weapons.

**Fate:** He was captured in 1960 and sent to prison for 25 years, but in 1964 he was **exchanged** for British spy Greville Wynne and returned to the Soviet Union.

# Physical disguise

## As part of their false identity, spies may use a physical disguise.

Spies should not attempt to totally transform their appearance. A 25-year-old trying to look like an old man aged 80 would not fool anyone, especially a security service agent.

▲ Wigs, glasses and a hat help to provide six different disguises for the same man.

## BASIC DISGUISE

The CIA gives its agents a basic disguise kit, including hair dye, false moustaches, cold cream and make-up. The kit also includes heel inserts to change the way a person walks. Such physical disguises are easy to use and will work in most situations.

◀ A range of rubber face parts used by the CIA, including a complete lower face.

# A COMPLETE DISGUISE

CIA's disguise expert Antonio Mendez helped six U.S. **diplomats** escape from Iran during the 1979 hostage crisis. Mendez disguised the Americans as members of a Canadian film crew who were preparing for a film to be shot in Iran. The U.S. **Consul General** was disguised as an eccentric film director with gold jewelry and tight trousers.

## Top Secret!

Everyone has their own way of walking and they can easily be identified by this. Developing a new walking style is one of the best secret-agent disguises.

CIA master of disguise Antonio Mendez shows his techniques to some schoolchildren.

As well as a physical disguise, Mendez coached the diplomats in how to talk and behave as a film crew. To create a convincing cover, he also set up a fake film company and paid for advertisements to appear in film magazines.

Mendez has now written two books about his experiences at the CIA—*Master of Disguise* and *Spy Dust*.

# Dead drops and concealment

**A dead drop is a place where spies and their handlers can leave or pick up money, information and equipment, without meeting each other.**

Dead drops are common in the spying world because they are less obvious than face-to-face meetings. The place chosen for the drop—sometimes called the **dead letter box**—must be easy to find, but allow the agent to pick up the item without arousing suspicion.

► *Typical locations might include a loose brick in a wall or hole in a tree, or the object might be taped underneath a park bench or bridge.*

## SETTING SIGNALS

A series of signals, such as chalk marks on a fence, will tell the spy that a drop is to take place. American Aldrich Ames, who spied for the KGB, used drinks cans to signal his dead drops.

► *A note from the American spy Aldrich Ames to his Soviet handler, arranging a dead drop.*

I AM READY TO MEET AT B ON 1 OCT. I CANNOT READ NORTH 13-19 SEPT. IF YOU WILL MEET AT B ON 1 OCT PLS SIGNAL NORTH OF 20 SEPT TO CONFI. NO MESSAGE AT PIPE. IF YOU CANNOT MEE. 1 OCT, SIGNAL NORTH AFTE 27 SEPT WITH MESSAGE AT PIPE.

# WIRELESS DEAD DROP

In January 2006, Russian intelligence accused Britain's MI6 of using a hollowed-out rock for a **wireless** dead drop. According to the Russians, the spy would walk by the rock and send information from a hand-held device to the receiver in the rock. The information would be picked up by another spy using a hand-held device.

Russian television pictures claim to show a British spy leaving a hollow rock to be used as a wireless dead drop.

## DEAD-DROP SPECIALIST

An **FBI** double agent, Robert Hanssen spied for Soviet intelligence for more than 20 years. Hanssen was an expert at making dead drops, carefully choosing the locations himself and developing complex codes to arrange the drops.

He made 20 dead drops in various Virginia parks before being caught by the FBI in 2001. Hanssen wrapped up his material in waterproof plastic and fixed the bundles to the underside of bridges. The Soviets paid him $1.4 million for his information.

Hanssen used a bridge at Foxstone Park, Virginia, as a drop site.

# Surveillance

**The world of spy** surveillance **ranges from space satellites looking down on Earth to teams of watchers monitoring people in their cars or homes**.

Recent developments in technology have improved the ability to watch or listen in on a person or organization. Tracking devices, for example, can be fitted secretly to a suspect's car or even in their clothes or luggage.

▲ *The view from a surveillance camera, a 24-hour watcher of the streets below.*

## Top Secret!

Soviet mole Anthony Blunt was responsible for MI5's visual surveillance techniques. He passed on this information to his KGB handlers, helping Soviet agents escape British watchers.

Sometimes, it is necessary to simply watch the enemy spy closely. Security organizations, such as the FBI and MI5, have teams of watchers—specially trained people who can use their detailed knowledge of spy behavior to observe a suspect.

# CAMERAS

Miniature video cameras, webcams and closed-circuit televisions (CCTV) provide 24-hour visual surveillance of many important public areas. Some people believe, however, that there are too many of these cameras, and that they intrude into our lives.

➤ *Modern video cameras have become so small that they can be hidden in a person's clothes, or in the hand.*

# THE POWER OF ECHELON

Echelon is the code name for a surveillance system operated by the United States and supported by its allies, including Britain. Although a top-secret project, it is believed that Echelon can **intercept** and read most electronic communication, including phone calls, faxes, e-mails and Internet downloads.

In order to avoid information overload the system will pick up selected words, such as al-Qaeda or suicide bomber, from specific target locations. Originally designed to target the Soviet Union, it is now used against a variety of targets, including terrorist and drug-running organizations.

Echelon may intercept up to three billion communications every day.

17

# Tailing and shaking a tail

An FBI surveillance photo of a Soviet agent (in tracksuit) with Richard Miller (dark trousers), who sold FBI secrets to the Soviets.

**Tailing or shadowing someone is an important part of spy tradecraft.**

Any experienced secret agent will know how to follow an unsuspecting person without being noticed. An agent will also be taught to know if they are being followed and how to shake off the tail.

## TAILING

Tailing is normally carried out in a car or on foot. Both are far more effective if they are done in teams, especially when equipped with radios. Whether in a car or on foot, team members take turns to follow the suspect, who then finds it very difficult to work out if there is someone following them.

## Top Secret!

Frank Brossard was a Soviet spy who worked at the British air ministry. He was caught by MI5 when they put a tracking device within some top-secret papers that he took to photograph.

18

# SHAKING A TAIL

Secret agents find out about and shake off tails in different ways. In a car, they might signal to move in one direction and then suddenly drive straight on. In a car or on foot, the spy will take several left or right turns, one after another. Anyone following their unusual route would then look suspicious.

Tailing a car. Modern tracking devices and satellite navigation systems make this a much easier business.

When getting off a train, bus or underground train, the spy will slip out at the very last moment as the doors are closing. The tail will now be left to carry on in the train or bus. If anyone jumps out with the spy, they will almost certainly be a tail.

In the film The Bourne Identity, the hero is tracked across Europe by rogue secret-service agents.

# Black-bag operations

A spy breaks into a locked office to steal or photograph enemy top-secret documents.

**A black-bag operation is the secret entry into an office or home to steal or copy materials.**

This is an illegal and risky business because if caught, the intelligence organization that has ordered the operation might be in trouble with its own government.

The FBI carried out black-bag operations against Japanese **consular** offices in the United States during the 1920s and 1930s. The Japanese were unaware of these break-ins, which supplied U.S. intelligence with vital information about Japanese codes.

In 1955, MI5 secretly broke into a house in London, England, that held membership files of the **Communist Party** in Britain. MI5 removed the files, photographed them and returned them without anyone knowing of the break-in. All security services carry out black-bag operations at some point.

# WATERGATE SCANDAL

The most famous black-bag operation
went disastrously wrong. It involved
a break-in at the Watergate complex
in Washington D.C. by secret agents
in 1972. They had been hired by the
U.S. **Republican Party** to spy on their
**Democratic Party** opponents.

During the break-in, the black-bag team was
spotted and arrested by local police. When the
operation was revealed, it eventually led to the
resignation of the U.S. President, the Republican
Richard M. Nixon.

A view of the Watergate complex
in Washington D.C., scene of the
black-bag operation.

21

# Black propaganda

**Black propaganda is false information where the source is deliberately disguised. It will seem to come from one side in a conflict but, in fact, comes from the other side.**

In World War II, the British set up Radio Deutschland, which claimed to be a German forces radio station, but actually **broadcast** anti-**Nazi** messages. The broadcasts were so clever that they fooled many German listeners.

▲ British journalist Sefton Delmar broadcasts black propaganda to the Germans during World War II.

▲ Black propaganda was used against Iraqi dictator Saddam Hussein.

## RADIO TIKRIT

In February 2003, a station called Radio Tikrit began broadcasting in Iraq. At first it gave strong support to the Iraqi leader Saddam Hussein. As the war with the United States began, it started to criticize Hussein and the Iraqi government, and encouraged Iraqi soldiers to disobey orders. The radio station had, in fact, been set up by the CIA to lower the confidence of Iraqi soldiers.

# THE ZINOVIEV LETTER

Soviet leader Grigori Zinoviev, best known in Britain for his supposed call for revolution.

In 1924, a letter was published in the British *Daily Mail* newspaper. It was thought to have been sent by top Soviet communist, Grigori Zinoviev, to the Communist Party of Great Britain. The letter asked British communists to create trouble within the British **Labour Party** and the armed forces.

The letter was actually a fake made by a group in MI6 who wanted to make people distrust the Labour Party. It seemed to work—in the **General Election**, which was held four days afterward, Labour lost heavily to the **Conservatives**.

## Top Secret!

Some people thought that Zinoviev might become leader of the Soviet Union, but Joseph Stalin did instead. Zinoviev was arrested and shot for treason in 1936.

# Interrogation

**When spies are caught, their fate can be grim. They will face a long, detailed interrogation. In some situations, they may also be** tortured**.**

In order to get information, the spy's captors promise good treatment if the spy co-operates, but threaten severe punishment if they refuse.

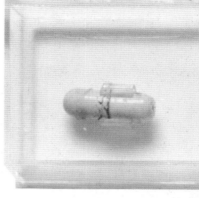

⬆ *Some spies carry deadly cyanide pills, to be used to prevent them breaking down under torture.*

⬆ *Handcuffs and a baton—some of the tools that a spy may face under interrogation.*

A range of methods will be used to make the spy talk— non-stop questioning by teams of interrogators, stopping the spy from sleeping, surrounding them with **white noise** and changing the temperature from very hot to cold. If these techniques do not work, then some interrogators move on to beating and other forms of physical torture.

Spies are trained to say nothing at first. If pushed, they are told to reveal some real information to please the interrogator, but the information will only help the captor a little. In the end, few people can cope with heavy interrogation. Some spies may commit suicide to avoid giving away secrets, or may agree to work for the enemy.

▌ *A captured secret agent will be held in a cell like this one in Fresnes prison, Paris. Many French Resistance prisoners were held there by the Germans during World War II.*

## Top Secret!

During World War II, British intelligence officers used a trick to make German prisoners talk. One prisoner would be taken behind a truck and a shot fired. The other prisoner would become scared and talk. The trick was that the gun had only been fired at the ground.

# Escape and evasion

**Spying is dangerous, and knowing when to stop is important to a spy's survival. If they leave it too late, they could face a painful interrogation with worse to come.**

Evasion is where a spy gets away before being caught. It is always better than escape, where a spy flees after being caught. Soviet spy Kim Philby used evasion when he heard from U.S. intelligence that accusations were being made against fellow Cambridge spy, Donald Maclean. Philby told Maclean, who fled to the Soviet Union with another Cambridge spy Guy Burgess — just ahead of MI5.

▲ Clockwise from the top left, the Cambridge spies: Anthony Blunt, Donald Maclean, Guy Burgess and Kim Philby.

In 1970, Polish intelligence officer Ryszard Kuklifski secretly rebeled against the Soviet domination of his country. He began sending documents of Soviet military strengths and intentions to the West. After ten years of spying, he realized that he was in real danger of being caught. His CIA handlers also realized the danger — Kuklifski and his family were hidden in a car and taken to safety in West Germany.

# PRISON BREAK

American Christopher Boyce was caught spying for the KGB. He escaped from prison in January 1980 and went on the run for 19 months, during which time he robbed at least 13 banks.

◄ KGB spy Christopher Boyce is closely guarded on his way from the courthouse to prison.

# GEORGE BLAKE'S ESCAPE

Double agent George Blake worked for MI6, while providing the KGB with information on Western intelligence agencies. He was arrested in 1961 and sentenced to 42 years in Wormwood Scrubs prison, London, England.

Blake was helped by other prisoners to break out in October 1966. Then former prisoners packed him into a van and drove him across Europe to East Germany. He was flown to Moscow, where he spent the rest of his life, with British spies, Maclean and Philby.

▲ George Blake, one of the few captured spies who managed to escape and get away to safety.

# Intelligence blunders

**No matter how experienced and well trained spies are, plans do not always run smoothly.**

Sometimes they trust the wrong people, or intelligence turns out to be fake. Or they may not trust the information that they are given, which turns out to be right.

Before the Germans invaded the Soviet Union in June 1941, Soviet spies had told Soviet leader Joseph Stalin that an attack would happen soon. Stalin refused to believe them until German tanks had smashed through the Soviet border.

▲ KGB spy Leopold Trepper's belief that Germany was about to invade the Soviet Union, but was ignored by Joseph Stalin.

In 1941, FBI leader J. Edgar Hoover ignored the warnings of Yugoslav spy Dusan Popov. He told Hoover that the Germans and Japanese were showing a special interest in the U.S. naval base at Pearl Harbor, but nothing was done. A few months later, on December 7, 1941, the Japanese launched a surprise attack on Pearl Harbor.

◄ Sinking U.S. warships at Pearl Harbor, following the surprise Japanese attack on December 7, 1941.

# THE BERLIN TUNNEL

After World War II, the city of Berlin was divided into Western and Soviet parts. In 1954, the CIA and MI6 began work on a tunnel that ran underneath the Soviet section. They wanted to tap into underground telephone lines that ran from the Soviet Military HQ in Berlin to Moscow and the rest of Germany.

The work was successful and a lot of Soviet military information was received in the West. It seemed a great victory for the CIA and MI6, but George Blake, a Soviet spy in MI6, had informed the KGB about the plan before the tunnel had even been built. The Soviets let the West listen in to unimportant military data before closing down the tunnel in 1956. It was only when Blake was caught in 1961 that the West realized they had been tricked.

*A scene inside the tunnel, stretching deep into the Soviet zone of Berlin.*

29

# GLOSSARY

**Assassinate** To kill others for political reasons.

**Broadcast** To send out by radio or television signals.

**CIA** Central Intelligence Agency, the intelligence-collecting organization of the United States.

**Communist Party** A political group that believes in a system based on the idea that the government owns and controls all property.

**Conservatives** Members of a political group, the British Conservative Party.

**Consular** A diplomat who helps people of their country while in a foreign country.

**Consul General** The head of the group of consular staff.

**Courier** A member of a spy ring who carries secret information from place to place, usually without knowing what it is.

**Cover story** A false story or identity used by spies to cover up their spying activities.

**Dead drop** A place where a spy leaves secret material to be picked up by a controller or another spy.

**Dead letter box** A secret and safe place where information is left during a dead drop.

**Defector** A person who has decided to work for an opposing country or intelligence organization.

**Democratic Party** A U.S. political group.

**Diplomat** A person who represents their own country to the government of another country. They will normally work from their embassy in the foreign country.

**Diplomatic status** Spies working directly from their embassy abroad are given special privileges that mean they cannot be imprisoned or executed if they are caught spying.

**Double agent** A spy working for two intelligence organizations at the same time. The spy is loyal to one side and pretending to be loyal to the other.

**Embassy** The offices of a country's diplomatic staff in a foreign country.

**Espionage** Spying to find out information.

**Exchange** The act of giving something to someone and receiving something in return.

**FBI** Federal Bureau of Investigation, the security service of the United States.

**Forgery** A copy of a document or letter to fool people into thinking it is genuine.

**General Election** An election, in which the people of the United Kingdom vote for the government of their choice.

**Government** A group of people who rule a country or state.

**Handler** Another word for a controller—an agent who directs and supports spies working undercover.

**Hostile country** A country belonging to the enemy.

**Intelligence** Secret information, or an organization that seeks secret information.

**Intercept** To stop something going from one place to another.

**Interrogate** To question a person so they supply information, whether willingly or unwillingly.

**KGB** The combined security and intelligence services of the Soviet Union.

**Labour Party** A British political group.

**MI5** Military Intelligence Section 5, the security service of Great Britain.

**MI6** Military Intelligence Section 6, the intelligence service of Great Britain.

**Nazi** A member of the political group founded by Adolf Hitler, which ruled Germany from 1933 to 1945.

**Occupied** Under another country's control.

**Republican Party** A U.S. political group.

**Resistance** A secret organization that attacks an occupying army using tactics such as sabotage.

**SOE** Special Operations Executive, an undercover special operations and sabotage organization set up by Britain to attack the Germans in Occupied Europe.

**Soviet** Relating to a country in Europe and Asia, between 1917 and 1991.

**Surveillance** Watching something carefully.

**Torture** To cause serious pain as a punishment or to make someone do something.

**Tradecraft** The special techniques used by spies.

**West** Referring to the United States and its allies in Western Europe.

**Wireless** Without a cable or wire between sender and receiver.

**White noise** A sound used during interrogations to confuse the suspect.

# INDEX